Up-Grade!

Light relief between grades

Spaß und Entspannung mit leichten Originalstücken für Trompete
Erster Schwierigkeitsgrad

Plaisir et détente avec des pièces originales simples pour trompette
Niveau 1

Pamela Wedgwood

Contents

FABER *ff* MUSIC

Foreword

Up-Grade! is a collection of new pieces and studies in a wide variety of styles for trumpeters of any age. This book is designed to be especially useful to students who have passed Grade 1 and would like a break before plunging into the syllabus for Grade 2.

Whether you're looking for stimulating material to help bridge the gap between grades, or simply need a bit of light relief, I hope you'll enjoy *Up-Grade!*

Pamela Wedgwood

© 2001 by Faber Music Ltd
First published in 2001 by Faber Music Ltd
3 Queen Square London WC1N 3AU
Cover illustration by John Levers
Music set by Jackie Leigh
Printed in England by Caligraving Ltd
All rights reserved

ISBN 0-571-52131-2

To buy Faber Music publications or to find out about the full range of titles available please contact your local music retailer or Faber Music sales enquiries:

Faber Music Limited, Burnt Mill, Elizabeth Way, Harlow, CM20 2HX England
Tel: +44 (0)1279 82 89 82   Fax: +44 (0)1279 82 89 83
sales@fabermusic.com   www.fabermusic.com

1. Take It Easy

Pamela Wedgwood

2. The Huntsman's Song

Pamela Wedgwood

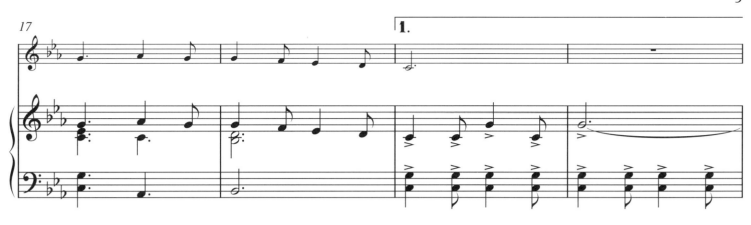

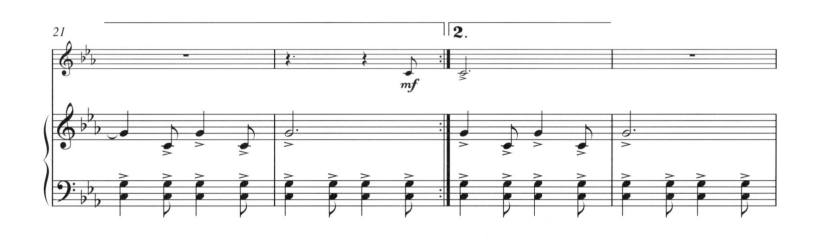

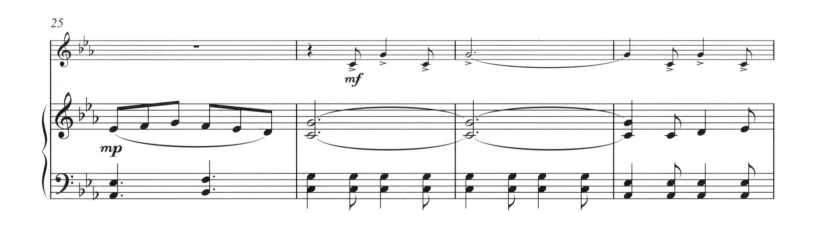

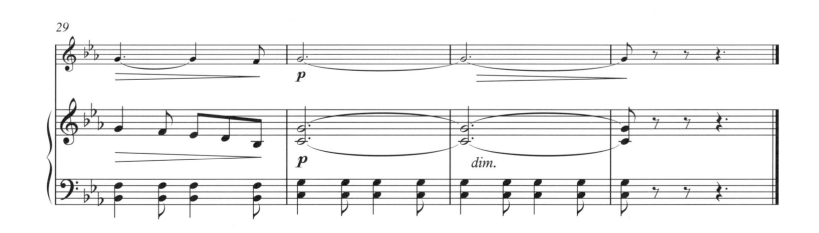

3. Apple Pie Waltz

Relaxed and sugary ♩ = 104

Pamela Wedgwood

rit. a tempo

4. I Believe

Pamela Wedgwood

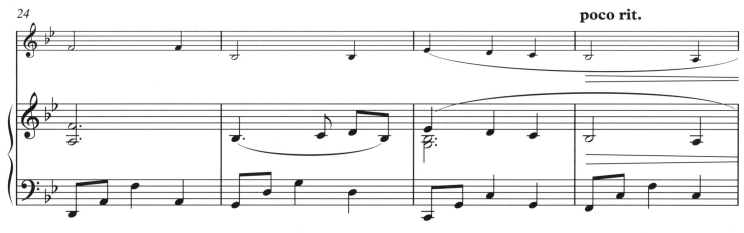

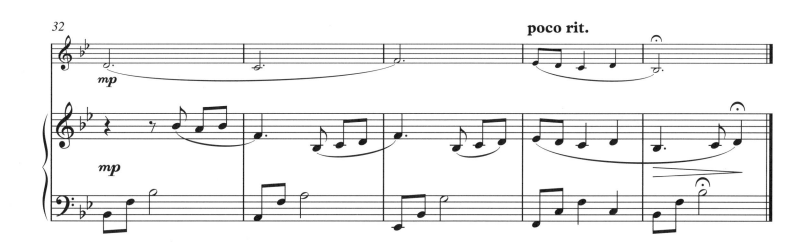

5. Over the sea to Skye

Traditional Scottish

6. Coconut Calypso

Pamela Wedgwood

With a moderately gentle breeze ♩ = 112-120

D. 𝄋 al Fine

7. Mexican Chilli Out

Pamela Wedgwood

37

41

8. Golden Eye

Pamela Wedgwood

Moderately – with a strong beat ♩ = 120

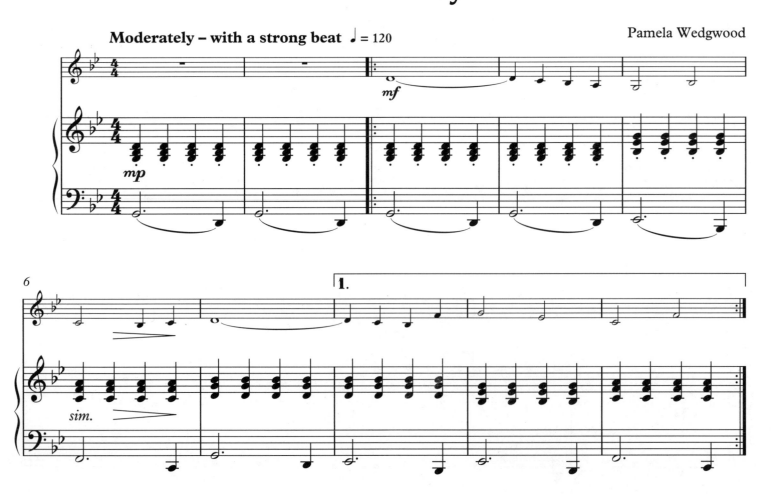

9. See, the Conquering Hero Comes

G.F. Handel
(1685-1759)
arr. Pamela Wedgwood

10. Internet Blues

Pamela Wedgwood

With a tired feeling – relaxed ♩ = 80-84

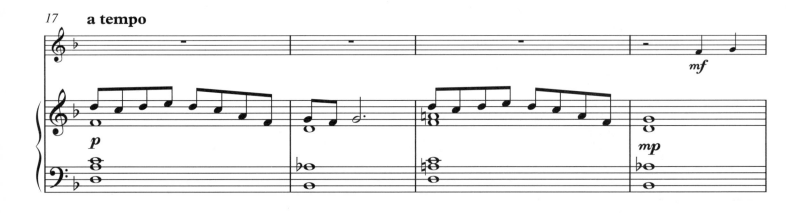

11. La donna è mobile

Giuseppe Verdi
(1813-1901)

12. Road Hog

Pamela Wedgwood

Fine

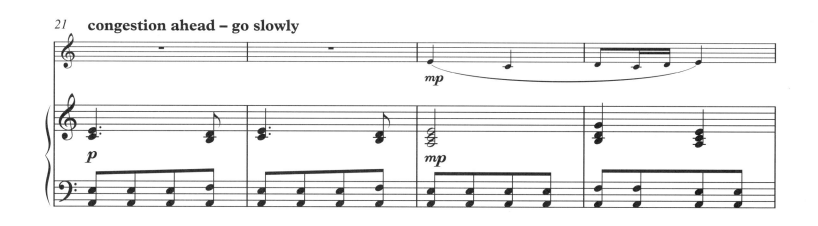

congestion ahead – go slowly

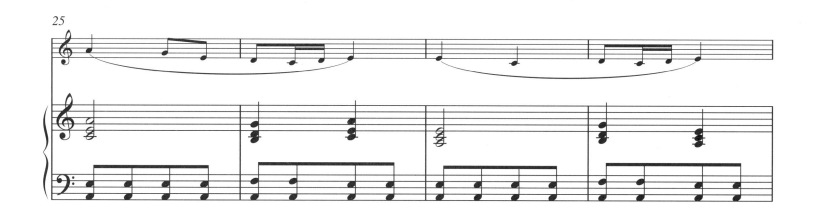

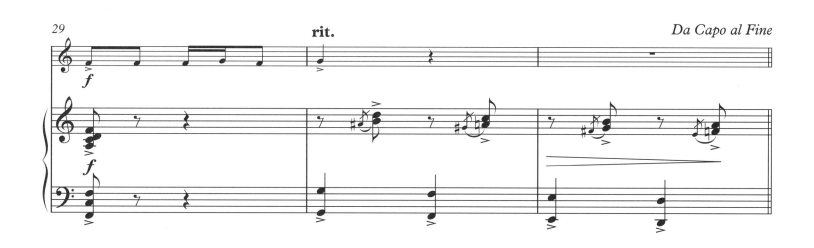

rit.

Da Capo al Fine

Up-Grade!

Light relief between grades

Spaß und Entspannung mit leichten Originalstücken für Trompete
Erster Schwierigkeitsgrad

Plaisir et détente avec des pièces originales simples pour trompette
Niveau 1

Pamela Wedgwood

Contents

FABER *ff* MUSIC

Foreword

Up-Grade! is a collection of new pieces and studies in a wide variety of styles for trumpeters of any age. This book is designed to be especially useful to students who have passed Grade 1 and would like a break before plunging into the syllabus for Grade 2.

Whether you're looking for stimulating material to help bridge the gap between grades, or simply need a bit of light relief, I hope you'll enjoy *Up-Grade!*

Pamela Wedgwood

© 2001 by Faber Music Ltd
First published in 2001 by Faber Music Ltd
3 Queen Square London WC1N 3AU
Cover illustration by John Levers
Music set by Jackie Leigh
Printed in England by Caligraving Ltd
All rights reserved

ISBN 0-571-52131-2

To buy Faber Music publications or to find out about the full range of titles available
please contact your local music retailer or Faber Music sales enquiries:

Faber Music Limited, Burnt Mill, Elizabeth Way, Harlow, CM20 2HX England
Tel: +44 (0)1279 82 89 82   Fax: +44 (0)1279 82 89 83
sales@fabermusic.com   www.fabermusic.com

1. Take It Easy

Gently ♩ = 88

Pamela Wedgwood

mf *p* *mf* *p*

2. The Huntsman's Song

Lively

Pamela Wedgwood

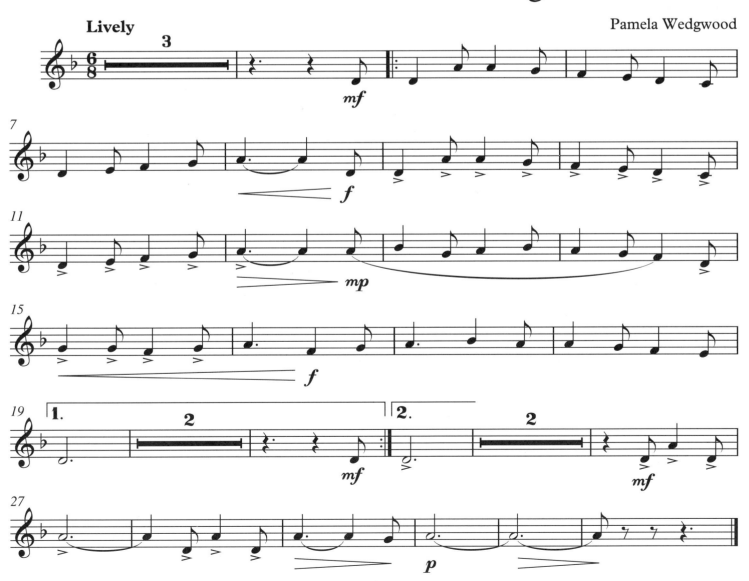

mf *f* *mp* *f* *mf* *mf* *p*

4

3. Apple Pie Waltz

Pamela Wedgwood

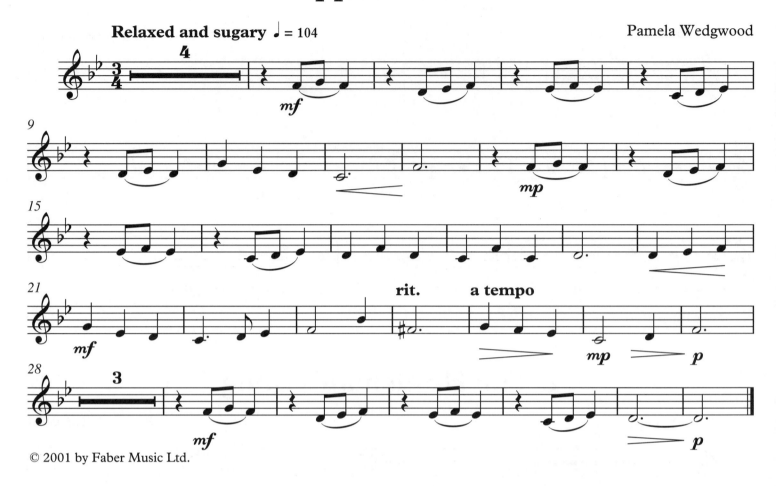

4. I Believe

Pamela Wedgwood

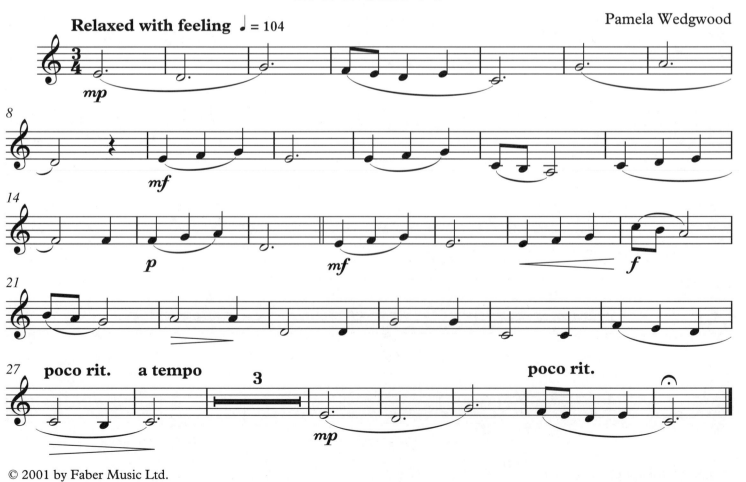

5. Over the sea to Skye

Simply ♩ = 88

Traditional Scottish

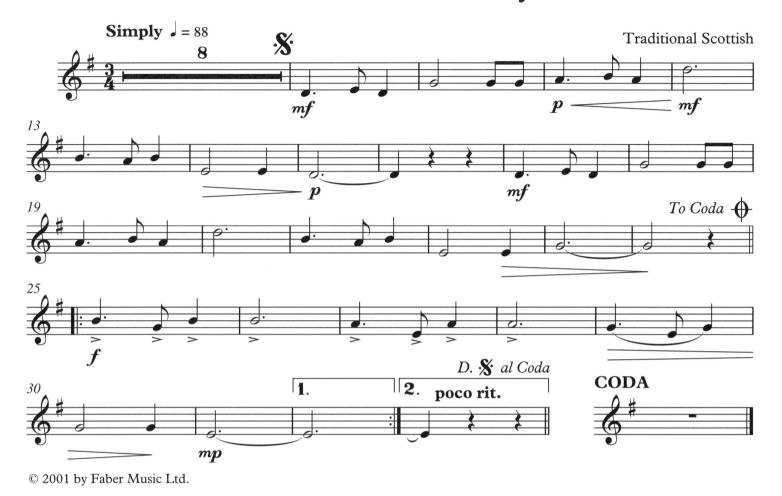

6. Coconut Calypso

With a moderately gentle breeze ♩ = 112–120

Pamela Wedgwood

7. Mexican Chilli Out

Bossa Nova – very relaxed ♩ = 132

Pamela Wedgwood

8. Golden Eye

Moderately – with a strong beat ♩ = 120

Pamela Wedgwood

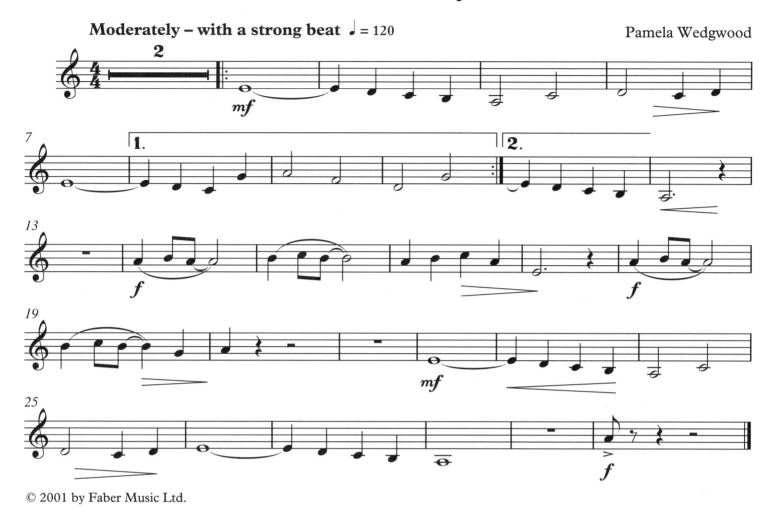

© 2001 by Faber Music Ltd.

9. See, the Conquering Hero Comes

G.F. Handel
(1685-1759)
arr. Pamela Wedgwood

At a brisk marching speed ♩ = 116

© 2001 by Faber Music Ltd.

10. Internet Blues

With a tired feeling – relaxed ♩ = 80-84

Pamela Wedgwood

11. La donna è mobile

Giuseppe Verdi
(1813-1901)

Allegretto ♩ = 120

12. Road Hog

Pamela Wedgwood

13. Monster-ous (Duets)

1. Rhino Rag

Pamela Wedgwood

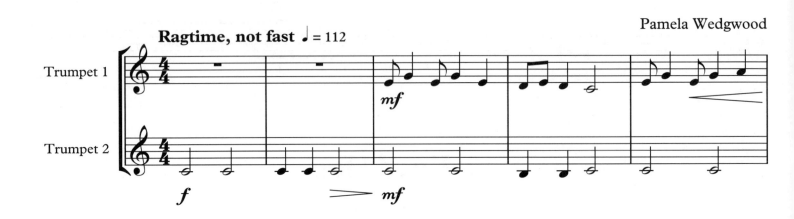

2. Hippo Hop

Pamela Wedgwood

3. Crocodile Crunch

Pamela Wedgwood

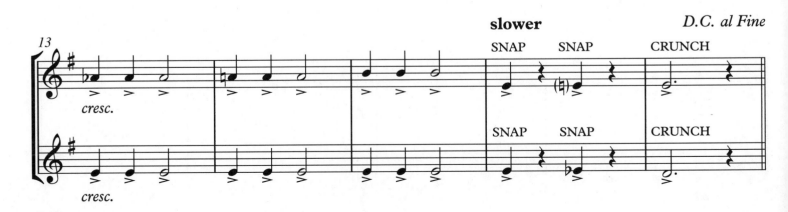